A GUIDE TO
ZUNI FETISHES
AND CARVINGS

VOLUME II: THE MATERIALS AND THE CARVERS

by Kent McManis

Photography by Robin Stancliff

TREASURE CHEST BOOKS
TUCSON, ARIZONA

ACKNOWLEDGMENTS

This book could not have been completed without the help of many people. First and foremost, my eternal appreciation and love to my wife, Laurie, who has done so much to support me and make this work possible. Special thanks to Corilee Sanders and Micheal Dunham for their knowledge, their friendship, and pointing the way; this project owes a great deal to them. Special gratitude goes to Shirley Leekela-Baca at the Pueblo of Zuni Census Office for all the assistance in putting together the family trees. I could never have completed them without her and her staff. Thanks to Chet Jones for all the materials background and Sarah Leekya and especially Rena Othole for putting me in touch with the right people; to Don Sharp for his wit and all these years of answering my myriad questions; to Joe Douthitt for help with certain family trees; to Pat Harrington, Alice Killackey, Boyd Walker, and Scott Ryerson for historical data; to Denise Homer, Elaine Lesarlley, and Kit South for carver and family aid; and to Dick and Olga Anson and Bob Jones for help with carving materials. More applause for Robin Stancliff for bringing out the beauty in the fetishes. Gratitude to my dad for starting me down this long, Native American trail. And finally, to the many, many Zuni people who have been so generous with their knowledge, their guidance, their patience, their spirit, and their talent: E'lah:kwa!

TREASURE CHEST BOOKS
P. O. Box 5250
Tucson, AZ 85703-0250
(520) 623-9558

ISBN   1887896-11-2

Title page photo: fetish by Clive Hustito, lepidolite mountain lion

All fetishes pictured are courtesy of Grey Dog Trading Co. and private collections except the necklace on page 36 which is courtesy of Black Rock Trading Co.

This book is set in Bitstream Charter and ITC Goudy Sans typefaces.
Edited by Linnea Gentry
Designed by Paul Mirocha
Printed in Korea

CONTENTS

CARVING MATERIALS

WHEN I WROTE THE FIRST VOLUME of *A Guide to Zuni Fetishes and Carvings,* I wanted it to be a small useful book packed with as much practical information as possible. Even then I thought a second volume would be needed. Since its publication, I have been asked many questions about the materials that fetishes are carved from and also about the many carvers not included in the first book due to space constraints. Hopefully, this new work will answer the questions about both of these subjects.

Regarding minerals and rocks (stones made up of multiple minerals), first let me state that I am not a geologist. Hence, I have usually avoided the chemical compositions and the more technical terms for the stones. I think most non-scientific readers prefer "calcite" to "$CaCO_3$" or "calcium carbonate."

My favorite Zuni expression for many stones that the carvers cannot easily identify is, "It's a rock." To the carver, the type of rock may not matter unless the fetish is to be a specific directional color (see Volume I) or they have a special order for a certain stone. Usually the artist carves whatever he or she has on hand or sees in a store and likes. Most carvers have favorites they work regularly. Of course, they try to find materials with eye appeal and interesting patterns that will make their fetishes easier to sell. Both collectors and artists especially admire a carver's ability to use natural markings to interesting advantage on a fetish. This is an undeniable part of the aesthetic appeal. A good example would be finding a piece of Picasso marble with a white stripe and carving it into a badger with the stripe running down the middle of its back, just like the real animal's markings. As more Zuni enter the field, competition drives artists to do finer and more unusual work and encourages them to try new mediums in hopes of attracting attention to their fetishes.

The range of materials now worked by Zuni fetish carvers is amazing. I have tried to show as many types as possible, as well as the varieties within certain types. The work of many artists not previously shown is displayed within, since a number of new carvers have started after Volume I was initially published.

ALABASTER

Hubert Pincion,
painted swan ˙

A TYPE OF GYPSUM, alabaster is a very soft material you can scratch with your fingernail. This softness makes it easy to work and, hence, a favorite for beginning fetish carvers. It comes in a variety of colors–white, reddish, brown, grey, orange, and green–which sometimes occur together in the same piece. Most types are opaque. Alabaster has been used for carving at Zuni for many years, much of it now coming from Colorado and Nevada. The white type is often used for white healing bears or east directional fetishes (see Volume I).

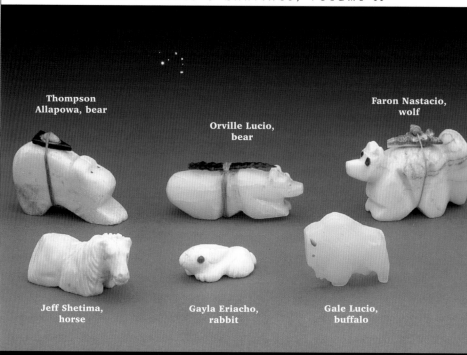

Thompson
Allapowa, bear

Orville Lucio,
bear

Faron Nastacio,
wolf

Jeff Shetima,
horse

Gayla Eriacho,
rabbit

Gale Lucio,
buffalo

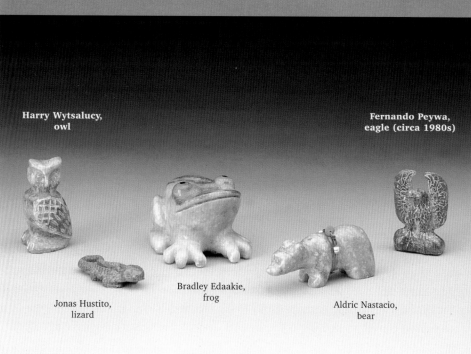

Harry Wytsalucy,
owl

Fernando Peywa,
eagle (circa 1980s)

Jonas Hustito,
lizard

Bradley Edaakie,
frog

Aldric Nastacio,
bear

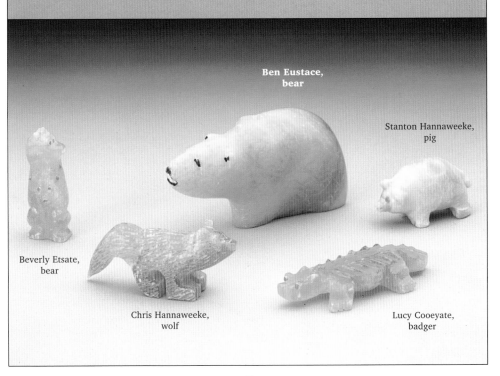

Jodi Edaakie,
frog

Tony Chopito,
buffalo

Stewart Lasiloo,
bear

Darren Zunie,
bobcat

Brian Yatsattie,
lizard

Ben Eustace,
bear

Stanton Hannaweeke,
pig

Beverly Etsate,
bear

Chris Hannaweeke,
wolf

Lucy Cooeyate,
badger

7

SERPENTINE

THE MINERAL SERPENTINE was used as early as prehistoric times for carving in the Southwest. It appears in a wide range of colors which include green, tan, grey, yellow, brown, pink, red, and creamy white, plus combinations of several hues in one stone. Serpentine is popular with beginning carvers because of its ready availability and general ease of carving. New Mexico and Arizona serpentines are most commonly worked in Zuni, where it is sold under many names, including "fish rock" (a light yellowish green), "frog rock" (a medium-light green with light green splotches and black veining), and ricolite (usually banded grey and green or dark green). Some dark serpentines are incorrectly sold as jade, which is much harder and considerably more expensive. Serpentine that contains other minerals as well goes by the name "serpentine marble." At Zuni, this includes what they call "red serpentine" and "chocolate serpentine." Opalized serpentine is a light greenish material that has been recently introduced in Zuni from Russia.

Anthony Mecale,
ricolite lizard

Terrance LaRue,
ricolite alligator

Kevin Chapman,
turtle

Yancy Robert Halusewa,
ricolite bear

Vinton Kallestewa,
ricolite bear

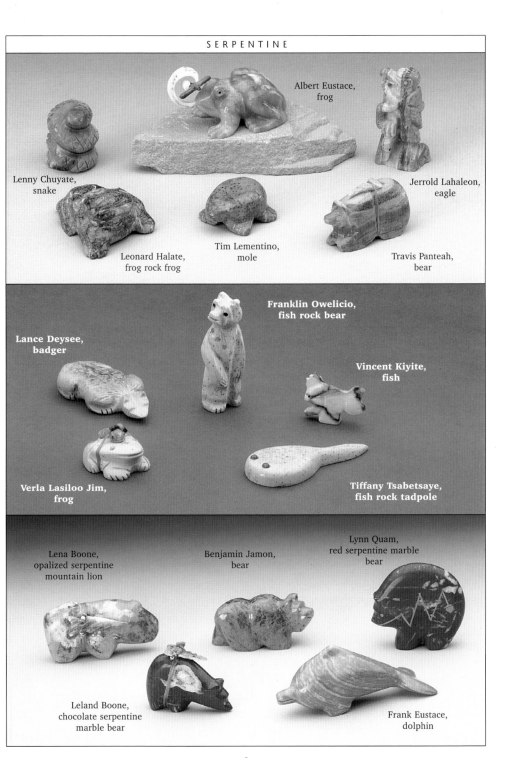

Lenny Chuyate,
snake

Albert Eustace,
frog

Jerrold Lahaleon,
eagle

Leonard Halate,
frog rock frog

Tim Lementino,
mole

Travis Panteah,
bear

**Lance Deysee,
badger**

**Franklin Owelicio,
fish rock bear**

**Vincent Kiyite,
fish**

**Verla Lasiloo Jim,
frog**

**Tiffany Tsabetsaye,
fish rock tadpole**

Lena Boone,
opalized serpentine
mountain lion

Benjamin Jamon,
bear

Lynn Quam,
red serpentine marble
bear

Leland Boone,
chocolate serpentine
marble bear

Frank Eustace,
dolphin

9

PICASSO MARBLE

Dana Malani,
bobcat

Sebastian Santos,
buffalo

PROBABLY THE MOST POPULAR rock being worked at Zuni today, Picasso marble is a type of limestone from southwestern Utah. Its popularity is due in part to the interesting patterning in tans, browns, greys, white, and black, hues that resemble the natural colors of many animals carved in fetish form. (The name came from the apparent similarity of its markings to the artwork of Pablo Picasso.) This material is relatively new to Zuni and has only been used there since the late 1980s. Carvers can get a fairly realistic-looking result if they choose and work their stone carefully. For directional animals, Picasso marble is sometimes used to represent the multi-colored fetishes of the sky.

Donovan Dewa,
bear

Jeff Eriacho,
bear

Harvey Ghahate,
bear

Shannon Garnaat,
bear

Farrell Kallestewa,
bear

Burt Awelagte,
bear

Chris Cellicion,
horse

Mike Leekela,
horse

Drucilla Martinez,
horse

Lenny Lonjose,
seal

Kane Etsate,
coyote

Stephan Lonjose,
snake

Nolan Laate,
bear

Saville Hattie,
wolf

Jazz Kiyite,
snake

Dana Etsate,
lizard

Dean Laselute,
frog

JET

Chico Booqua,
bear (c. 1980s)

JET (a hard black type of lignite coal) was used for jewelry and carvings in the Southwest in the prehistoric era, especially among the Anasazi people. Jet has been mined for centuries on what is now the Acoma Pueblo reservation near Zuni and is still found there today. Much of the jet now carved in Zuni also comes from Pennsylvania and even Africa. A difficult material to work, jet fractures easily in carving, is very messy, and is somewhat difficult to polish to a high shine. Silverado jet, an unusual variety that produces a "gun metal" sheen when properly polished, comes from Colorado. Some southwestern tribes consider jet a sacred stone.

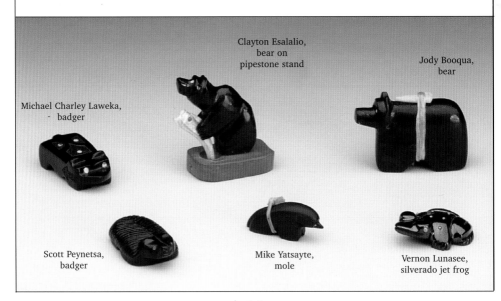

Clayton Esalalio,
bear on
pipestone stand

Jody Booqua,
bear

Michael Charley Laweka,
badger

Scott Peynetsa,
badger

Mike Yatsayte,
mole

Vernon Lunasee,
silverado jet frog

BLACK MARBLE

ANOTHER TYPE OF LIMESTONE, black marble comes primarily from Europe. It seems to have been introduced into Zuni relatively recently and has replaced the more challenging jet. Black marble accepts a much higher shine and has a glassier look when well polished. It's easy to distinguish from jet by its weight. A black fetish weighing next to nothing is probably jet, whereas a piece with some heft is more likely black marble. Because of its density, black marble provides a wonderful surface for sgrafitto carving. The Zuni often call this process "scratching" (see the Roselle Shack, Curtis Garcia, and Emerson Vallo pieces). Artisans usually choose either jet or black marble for the directional black fetishes of the underground (see Volume I).

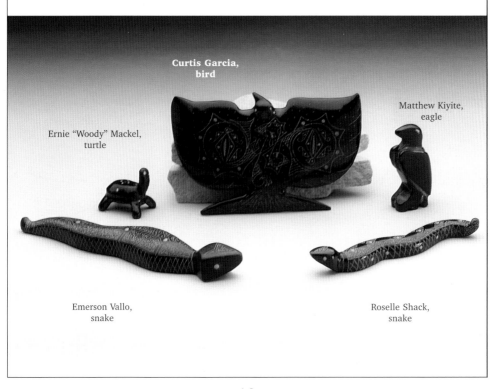

Curtis Garcia,
bird

Matthew Kiyite,
eagle

Ernie "Woody" Mackel,
turtle

Emerson Vallo,
snake

Roselle Shack,
snake

PIPESTONE

PIPESTONE (or, as it is known scientifically, catlinite) is basically a hardened clay mixture (also referred to as argillaceous rock) tinted red by iron. It is fairly simple to carve but can fracture easily during the process. The Plains Indians used catlinite to make the bowls of their ceremonial pipes (hence the name pipestone), and most of it came from Minnesota. The prehistoric peoples of the Southwest, however, used catlinite from central Arizona for their carving. Today, much of what the Zuni use still comes from Arizona, but some carvers also use Mid-western pipestone from both Minnesota and South Dakota. Catlinite was the first material used for the sgraffito process on fetishes (see Black Marble). Red fetish carvings for the south direction are often made from it (see Volume I).

Craig Lamy,
eagle

Harley Paquin,
wolf

James Cheama,
rabbit

Daphne Neha,
snake

Gerald Burns,
owl

Kenny Panteah,
snake

TURQUOISE AND RELATED MINERALS

Sarah Leekya,
turquoise bird

TURQUOISE is undoubtedly the stone most associated with Native Americans in the Southwest, and its use dates back to prehistoric cultures. While turquoise was worked by the ancient Hohokam peoples of southern Arizona, it found its fullest expression among the Anasazi people of the Colorado Plateau (now the Four Corners area of Arizona, New Mexico, Colorado, and Utah). These ancestors of present-day Pueblo Indians used turquoise in many types of jewelry as well as in fetish carving. It was traded in from mines as far away as the Mojave Desert in California, southern Nevada, the Kingman, Arizona, area, and southwestern New Mexico. The most famous prehistoric mine, however, was in Cerrillos, New Mexico, south of present-day Santa Fe. These ancient mines began as surface finds and later expanded to tunnel and open-pit mines.

Many Native Americans have considered it a sacred stone. The Zuni followed in their Anasazi ancestors' footsteps by carving turquoise and eventually setting it into silver jewelry as early as the 1890s. They often include turquoise in the bundle offerings attached to their fetishes. Before turquoise became readily available in the twentieth century, this was a rare and expensive "gift." At Zuni, crushed turquoise was served with blue corn meal as a traditional "food" for fetishes. It also appears in crushed form applied to the outside of communal fetish storage jars. Turquoise is often used to carve the blue fetish animals of the west direction (see Volume I).

Chemically, the mineral turquoise is a copper aluminum phosphate. The bluer the stone, the more copper it contains. The greener the stone, the more trace iron it has. Turquoise can be fairly soft (low grade) to relatively hard (high grade). Almost all of what the Zuni fetish carvers use is "stabilized" or "treated." This means a plastic or resin has been added to the stone to harden it (stabilize) or darken its color (treat). These processes allow carvers to work softer, lower grade, and thus less expensive stones. (In the old days, mutton fat or grease was used to treat stones.) Natural turquoise can fracture easily in carving, but some artists occasionally still carve natural stone as old-timers did. Much of the turquoise used today comes from Arizona, Nevada, Mexico, China, and Tibet. Stones from Colorado, New Mexico, Utah, and Australia appear much less frequently. Persian turquoise was imported for Native American jewelers as early as the 1890s.

Often found with turquoise in copper deposits, azurite (a deep blue mineral), malachite (a deep green mineral), and chrysocolla (a blue or green mineral) are its minerological cousins. These three often appear jumbled together in different combinations in the same rock. All of them were traditionally used for fetish carving at Zuni. Much of the combination material carved there today comes from Arizona; but the deep-green banded malachite worked by Zuni carvers is generally imported from the Congo. Some carvers shy away from it because the dust created during grinding can be harmful without proper ventilation.

Variscite is a greenish aluminum phosphate primarily from Utah and Nevada that is much less common in carved form. Other turquoise-related minerals are used for fetishes on very rare occasions.

Carol Martinez,
horse

Sarah Leekya,
frog

Donovan Laiwakete,
natural turquoise
horse

Marcus Panteah,
eagle

Fernando Laiwakete,
natural turquoise bear

Joey Quam,
covellite bear

**Debra Gasper and
Raymond Tsethlikai,
chrysocolla bear**

Jeffrey Tsalabutie,
variscite buffalo

Faylena Cachini,
variscite frog

Lloyd Lasiloo,
cobalt azurite bear

Andrew and Laura Quam,
azurite/malachite frog

DOLOMITE

Chris Pooacha,
lizard

DOLOMITE ROCK (another type of limestone, like marble) may appear banded, mottled, or fairly uniform in color. As seen in the examples here, much of it looks to me something like a thick milkshake with soft hues of yellow, pink, and sometimes reds. Solid brick red (often mistaken for pipestone) is also seen. Dolomite can also form as a mineral with white, red, pink, grey, yellow, or brown coloration. The Zuni carve mineral dolomite only on extremely rare occasions, usually preferring dolomite rock that comes from Mexico. Artists often carve the more yellowish dolomite for north directional fetishes and the multi-colored banded dolomite for directional fetishes of the sky (see Volume I).

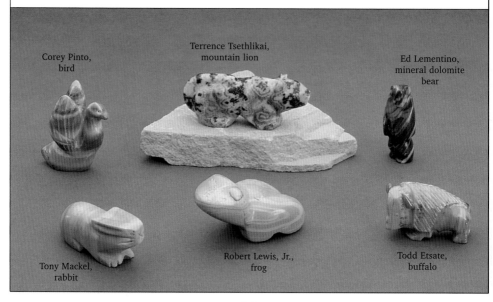

Corey Pinto,
bird

Terrence Tsethlikai,
mountain lion

Ed Lementino,
mineral dolomite
bear

Tony Mackel,
rabbit

Robert Lewis, Jr.,
frog

Todd Etsate,
buffalo

FLUORITE

ALTHOUGH MOST PREVALENT as a crystalline mineral, much of the fluorite used for fetish carving at Zuni is a massive (non-crystalline) variety called "purple fluorite." In this type, yttrium replaces some of the normal calcium that partly makes up fluorite. Massive purple fluorite is opaque, while regular fluorite is translucent or transparent. The latter comes in many different colors including white, yellow, aqua, blue, and brown as well as purple. Some multi-hued specimens are nicknamed "rainbow fluorite." Both types of fluorite worked at Zuni usually come from Mexico.

Terry Dishta,
purple fluorite
buffalo

Cellester Laate,
purple fluorite
corn maiden

Richard Epaloose,
purple fluorite bear

Donovan Chattin,
purple fluorite
corn maiden

Terrence Tsethlikai,
mountain lion

Bernard Homer, Jr.,
bear

Leland Boone,
frog

Rodney Laiwakete,
frog

Marlo Booqua,
rainbow fluorite double bears

MISCELLANEOUS STONES

NEW STONES FOR FETISH CARVING are constantly being introduced into the Zuni community. Some, because of ready availability, ease of carving, or attractive coloring, become favored materials for carvers. Others may be too expensive, too hard, or too scarce to be generally accepted. Many artists purchase carving materials from traders in Zuni or nearby cities. Stone merchants also bring stones directly to Zuni. The old days of searching the surrounding area for interesting rocks to carve are virtually over. This is due in part to the effort it takes to find such stones, which takes away time for carving. Mostly it is because the non-Native American purchasers of fetishes prefer more exotic and colorful stones than those usually found around the Zuni countryside. Also, some carvers simply enjoy the challenge of working with new and different mediums. While I have tried to be as comprehensive as possible, new stones are undoubtedly being introduced as you read this text. I have listed the areas of origin for the stones in common use at Zuni, although the stones may also be found in other parts of the world.

Blue and purple stones are fairly scarce but quite popular with fetish buyers. Sugilite (a manganese mineral introduced from South Africa around 1979), charoite (introduced from Russia in the 1970s), and lepidolite (traditionally worked by some Pueblo fetish carvers and found in New Mexico and California) are three purple minerals in use today. Lapis lazuli (from Afghanistan and Chile) and sodalite (a Bolivian mineral which is part of the composition of lapis lazuli) are two of the most popular blue stones. Sodalite differs from lapis in that it never has golden pyrite flecks. A lighter blue lapis lazuli called "denim lapis" is also catching on for fetishes. Bluish-grey materials in rare-to-occasional use include angelite (an anhydrite from Peru), labradorite (a feldspar from Madagascar), and Montana soapstone (a type of talc).

Green fetish materials are quite varied as well. Jade, steatite (another form of talc), septarian nodules (an olive-colored clay ironstone with yellow to whitish calcite crystals from Utah), gaspeite (a newly introduced apple-green nickel mineral associated with magnesite found in Australia), amazonite (a blue-green feldspar now coming from Russia), and aventurine (a muted green quartz from India) are all worked, but none of them with any regularity.

Yellow, brown, and orange stones used by the Zuni include yellow marble (a limestone variety), calcite (a mineral that appears in a myriad of colors, usually imported from Mexico), iron pyrite ("fool's gold"), brownish soapstone (from Colorado), tiger's eye (a yellow-brown quartz from South Africa), and brown obsidian (a natural glass used by some Native Americans, past and present, in the manufacture of arrowheads and points). Only calcite fetishes are seen frequently.

Red and pink materials are also quite popular with fetish buyers although, again, most are not common. Some of these are rhodochrosite (a bright pink mineral coming mostly from Argentina), rhodonite (a related but more muted pink mineral, with grey and black markings from Australia and Canada), alunite (a mineral from Colorado and Nevada), and "Ojo rock" (an argillaceous rock found on the Zuni Reservation near Ojo Caliente in colors from light pink to off-white).

White, transparent white, milky white, and black and white stones used for fetish carving include selenite (a crystalline gypsum from Utah), prystinite (a very rare mineral from the southwestern U.S.), opal, white marble, "zebra stone" or "skunk rock" (a black and white marble from Utah), and snowflake obsidian (a black and white obsidian also from Utah). All except "zebra stone" and selenite are rarely worked.

Banded materials are favored by fetish collectors because of their multi-hued colorations. The stone known as hickoryite or hickorite in the lapidary trade is

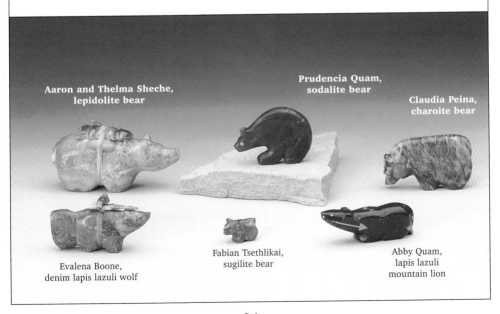

Aaron and Thelma Sheche, lepidolite bear

Prudencia Quam, sodalite bear

Claudia Peina, charoite bear

Evalena Boone, denim lapis lazuli wolf

Fabian Tsethlikai, sugilite bear

Abby Quam, lapis lazuli mountain lion

Aaron and Thelma Scheche,
angelite turtle

Prudencia Quam,
labradorite bear

Dan Simplicio,
soapstone bird

Lynn Quam,
aventurine bear

Lena Boone,
amazonite frog

also commonly called "wonderstone." It's a fine-grained rhyolite from Mexico. Other wonderstones from the western United States and banded sandstones are carved from time to time. (Plain grey or brown sandstone was a traditional fetish material at Zuni, but only a handful of carvers use it today.) Travertine, also known as "Mexican onyx," often has bands of white, yellow, red, brown, and pink and is a variety of calcite. Much of it is brought to Zuni from Arizona and Mexico. "Zuni stone" or "Zuni rock" is a massive (or, non-crystalline) travertine in yellow, brown, and grey hues found on the Zuni reservation. The late Leekya Deyuse (see Volume I) was especially noted for carving this stone; his descendents are virtually alone in continuing to do so today. Leekya and other older carvers also worked a dark brown, often banded agate from the Nutria area of the reservation called "Nutria rock." It is almost never in evidence today.

Another rock group used by fetish carvers is jasper (a type of fine-grained quartz) in a variety of coloration. The "leopard stone" variety has brownish spots over a lighter background (from Mexico) or a darker background (from Colorado). "Indian paint stone" comes from Nevada with tan, black, and brick red markings. Other jaspers come from many different locales, none of which are worked with great regularity.

**Herbert Him, Sr.,
steatite bear**

Terry Aisetewa,
jade lizard

Sarah Leekya,
gaspeite bird

Fernando Laiwakete,
brown obsidian bear

Faye Eriacho,
septarian bear

**Octavius Chuyate,
calcite coyote**

Lloyd Lasiloo,
tiger's eye horse

Dan Poncho,
marble horse

Joey Quam,
iron pyrite frog

Evalena Boone,
calcite mole

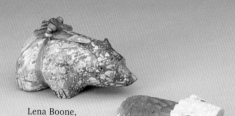

Lena Boone,
alunite badger

Leroy Chavez,
painted Ojo rock (argillaceous rock)
horned toad

Elroy Pablito,
rhodochrosite bear

Todd Westika,
rhodonite bear

Darrell Westika,
Arizona sandstone
bear

Leland Boone,
selenite bear

Fitz Kiyite, Jr.,
marble whale

Calvert Bowannie,
opal frog

Marlo Booqua,
prystinite
badger

Evalena Boone,
Utah sandstone
wolf

Danny Lonjose,
zebra stone
(marble) badger

Marlo Booqua,
snowflake obsidian
bear

Victor Martza,
zebra stone
(marble) snake

Georgette Quam
hickoryite (rhyolite) turtle

Francis Leekya,
Zuni stone
(travertine) bear

Hayes Leekya,
Zuni stone
(travertine) frog

Jimmie Etsate,
Mexican onyx bird

Leekya Deyuse,
Nutria rock
(agate) turtle

Terrence Tsethlikai,
Mexican onyx
mountain lion

Chris Yuselew,
onyx turtle

Leland Boone,
Indian paint stone
(jasper) bear

Rosella Lunasee,
Mexican leopard
stone (jasper)
mountain lion

Todd Chavez,
Indian paint stone
(jasper) dolphin

Marlo Booqua,
jasper bear

Debra Gasper and Raymond Tsethlikai,
Colorado leopard stone (jasper)
mountain lion

SHELL

SHELLS OF DIFFERENT TYPES were brought into the Southwest by overland trade routes during the prehistoric period, many from the Gulf of California (also known as the Sea of Cortez). Abalone and olivella (olive) shells were traded in from the coast of southern California. The Hohokam were the greatest users of shell for jewelry and fetish pendants including frogs, birds, and a range of animals. They also traded their surplus to the Mogollon people, who in turn supplied shells to the Anasazi of the Four Corners region. The Anasazi used shells but produced few fetishes from them. Some of the Pueblo peoples have often considered uncarved shells to be fetishes, however. The Zuni frequently mixed crushed shell with crushed turquoise and applied them to the outside coating of fetish storage jars.

Fetish bundle offerings have often included drilled shell beads called hishi (HEE-SHE). As with stones, a wide variety of shells from around the world are now available to the Zuni carver. White mother-of-pearl (the iridescent inside of the shell) is undoubtedly the most common. One variety has a band of yellow along the upper edge of the shell and is called "gold lip" mother-of-pearl. Green seasnail shell is another popular material showing an inner greyish pearlescence and occasional green and white colorations from the outside of the shell.

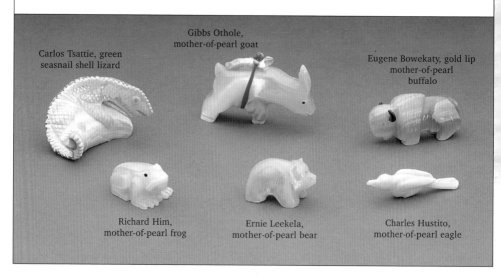

Gibbs Othole,
mother-of-pearl goat

Carlos Tsattie, green
seasnail shell lizard

Eugene Bowekaty, gold lip
mother-of-pearl
buffalo

Richard Him,
mother-of-pearl frog

Ernie Leekela,
mother-of-pearl bear

Charles Hustito,
mother-of-pearl eagle

Spondylus (spiny oyster) generally shows red, orange, or purple on the outside and white on the inside. Artists also experiment with different types of clam and conch shells. The main disadvantage in carving shell is from inhaling the grinding dust, so proper ventilation is imperative.

Schocke Sanchez,
penshell butterfly
on antler base

Sullivan Shebola,
olive shell duck

Fabian Homer,
abalone bear

Fabian Homer,
cowrie shell and
serpentine armadillo

Andrew and Laura Quam,
pink mussel shell frog

Mary Peina,
abalone bird
(c. 1960s)

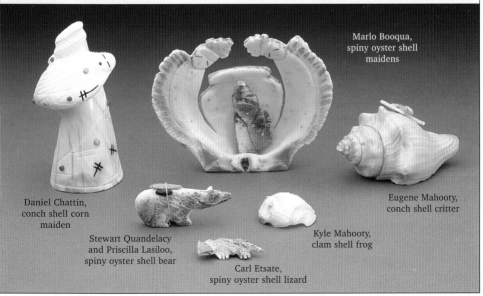

Marlo Booqua,
spiny oyster shell
maidens

Daniel Chattin,
conch shell corn
maiden

Stewart Quandelacy
and Priscilla Lasiloo,
spiny oyster shell bear

Carl Etsate,
spiny oyster shell lizard

Kyle Mahooty,
clam shell frog

Eugene Mahooty,
conch shell critter

ANTLER, HORN, FOSSILIZED IVORY, & BONE

ANTLER COMES PRIMARILY from deer and elk, although on rare occasions moose or caribou antler find their way into Zuni. Much of it is dropped by the animals themselves during their annual molting phase, but a goodly portion of the supply is brought into Zuni by traders. Its use dates to the prehistoric period. Water serpents, animals, and anthropomorphic figures on fetish pots were frequently made of antler. Sometimes these carvings were partly hollowed out to hold offerings and food for the fetishes. Antler is relatively soft but holds together fairly well in carving. It ranges from white to grey to yellowish, often with the grainy marrow revealed on the carving. Several fetish carvers known for detailed animals have made it their material of choice. The greatest drawback to antler is the odor, much like the smell of burning hair, produced when grinding it. Some artists deliberately burn antler to give it distinct brown areas.

Horn of different types—from domestic cows and goats to foreign water buffalo—is carved only rarely. The ivory seen today for fetishes is no longer elephant ivory, but fossilized ivory from Alaska. Bone is carved on occasion but was more frequently used in prehistoric times.

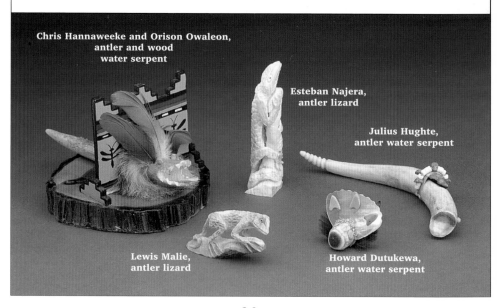

Chris Hannaweeke and Orison Owaleon,
antler and wood
water serpent

Esteban Najera,
antler lizard

Julius Hughte,
antler water serpent

Lewis Malie,
antler lizard

Howard Dutukewa,
antler water serpent

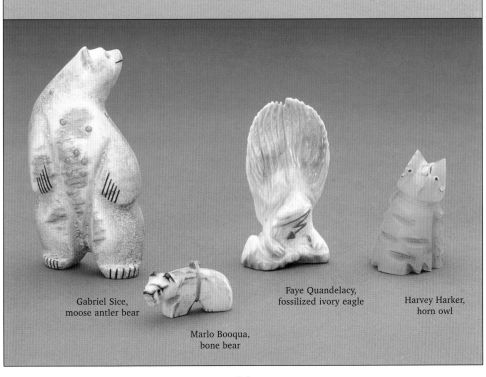

Destry Siutza,
antler eagle

Marlene Waikeniwa,
antler owl

Destry Siutza,
antler ducks

Howard Lesarlley,
antler owl

Elton Nastacio,
antler owl

Gabriel Sice,
moose antler bear

Marlo Booqua,
bone bear

Faye Quandelacy,
fossilized ivory eagle

Harvey Harker,
horn owl

OTHER ORGANIC MATERIALS

Marlo Booqua,
coral maiden and coyote

A LIVING UNDERSEA ORGANISM, coral was first imported into Zuni in the 1930s to be set into jewelry. Leekya Deyuse used it sparingly in his fetish carvings. Today coral has become very expensive due to over-harvesting in the Mediterranean and is now a rarity.

Amber is fossilized tree sap imported from both the Baltic region and the Dominican Republic. It is very lightweight, ranges from yellow to mottled brown, reddish, and gold, and may be clear or cloudy. Expensive, top-quality amber often has inclusions. It has become more popular for carving in recent years due to collector demand.

Another material whose use dates back to prehistoric times is wood. Although it is infrequently used today, sometimes cedar, ironwood, or local soft woods do appear in fetish form. Also uncommon, tagua nut (a palm nut from South America often called "vegetable ivory") was originally supplied to carvers as an alternative to ivory in the 1970s.

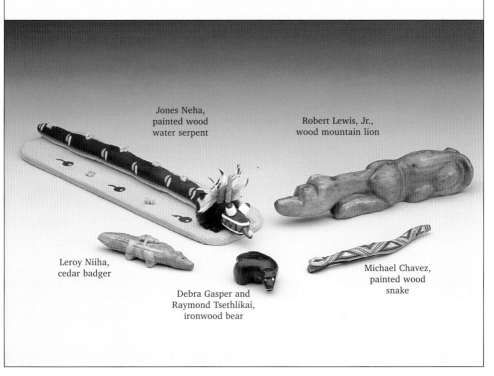

Andres Quandelacy,
amber buffalo

Avriel Lamy,
tagua nut
armadillo

Gibbs Othole,
amber bear

Fabian Tsethlikai,
coral bear head

Jones Neha,
painted wood
water serpent

Robert Lewis, Jr.,
wood mountain lion

Leroy Niiha,
cedar badger

Debra Gasper and
Raymond Tsethlikai,
ironwood bear

Michael Chavez,
painted wood
snake

31

GLASS

Leland Boone,
stained glass bear

GLASS IS A MATERIAL quite new to Zuni fetish carvers. Goldstone and bluestone are glass with copper. Gold slag is the glass residue left after gold is chemically removed from the ore. Stained glass has metallic oxides added to give the material its different colors. Among others, cobalt oxide is used to produce blue glass; copper oxide produces green glass; gold oxide makes red glass; tin oxide creates opaque white glass and makes other colors opaque; and lead mixtures can color yellow glass. Very few carvers are using glass to date because of the difficulty working it without special tools.

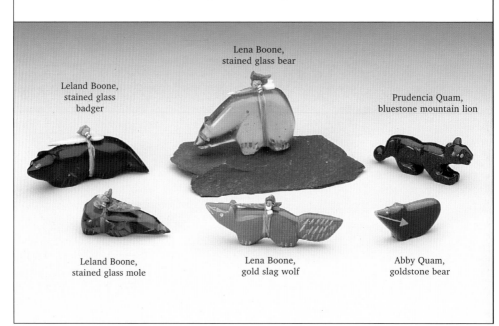

Lena Boone,
stained glass bear

Leland Boone,
stained glass
badger

Prudencia Quam,
bluestone mountain lion

Leland Boone,
stained glass mole

Lena Boone,
gold slag wolf

Abby Quam,
goldstone bear

ONE CARVER'S MATERIALS

CARVER RICKY LAAHTY, shown in the Leekya Deyuse family tree in Volume I, is known for his whimsical frogs. The examples shown here reveal how one carver can create the same animal repeatedly and yet still give each fetish its own personality. Ricky also gives us a good look at a wide range of the materials he selects to create visual interest in his work.

Picasso marble

turquoise

Nutria rock
(agate)

serpentine

natural turquoise

serpentine

azurite/malachite

green seasnail shell

rhodochrosite

spiny oyster
shell

alabaster

abalone

amber

leopard stone
(jasper)

THE CARVING FAMILIES

In the first volume, I covered four fetish-carving families at Zuni. While these four are important historically, there are other families with long carving traditions as well. In this volume, I have attempted to show many other carvers at Zuni and their extended families. Due to space limitations, I could not include all of these groups nor the many other talented carvers who are not in any of these families. All serious admirers of fetishes should be aware that new innovative artists are taking up the craft every year.

Certain points should be made about the family trees. It is not uncommon for a child of one family member to be adopted by a relative for a variety of reasons. Adoptions also occur among members of the same clan. Thus, strict bloodlines are not always represented in these trees. One Zuni may say he or she is not related to another, while that person may say they are. Whether or not the individual accepts adoption into a family and considers himself or herself "related" determines the point of view. In general I have tried to denote the adoptees' feelings by where they are placed in the tree. If parents appear in different charts, I have shown the children in the family of the mother. As in most contemporary societies, the Zuni sometimes change partners. The relationships portrayed here were what I knew as I compiled the trees. In addition, it is possible that I am unaware of the work of some individuals who may have carved a piece or two at one time or another.

In the trees that follow, the names of the carvers are shown in red and the names of the non-carvers in black. A (D) symbol means the individual is deceased. (1H) means first husband. (2H) means second husband. (1W) means first wife. (2W) means second wife. An equals (=) symbol means married or partners. A triangle (▲) means the carver is shown in more than one family.

I truly enjoyed assembling this chapter, as it enabled me to talk to so many wonderful Zuni people. At times it was like putting together a jigsaw puzzle, finding one piece of information here, another piece there. One interesting point is how the definitions of relationships differ from Anglo definitions, the term "aunt" being a good example. You may meet a young woman who is many years the junior of an elderly Zuni man, yet she says she is his "aunt." What she means to the non-Native American is that she is his religious "clan aunt" who helps him with certain observances and tasks. The word "cousin" is also unusual to outsiders, connoting anything from the person's blood cousin to step-brother to any distant relative to a fellow clan member. The interplay of the marked differences between Zuni and Anglo societies and of their many similarities is part of what made this project so fascinating.

Pernell Gasper,
jet and turquoise ram
(c. 1970s)

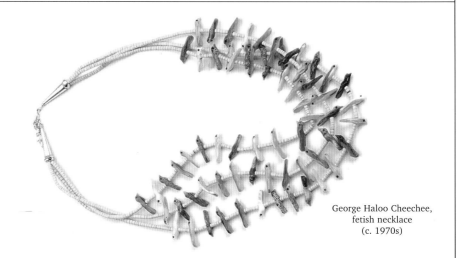

George Haloo Cheechee,
fetish necklace
(c. 1970s)

GEORGE HALOO (HAH-LOO) Cheechee is one of the most important figures in Zuni fetish carving. He passed on his knowledge to his extended family who in turn shared it with their families, relatives, and friends. Many other carving families on the pages that follow first learned from George or one of his descendents. He started carving in the 1930s and was known for his fetish necklaces, distinguished by the slightly turned heads of his animals. George died in 1983. He taught his daughter Lita Delena (DEH-LEE-NAH) who with her husband, Sam, have produced their own unique style of fetish necklaces since the 1960s. A few carvers on this side of the family create standing fetishes, but most were instructed in the making of stringing fetishes by Sam and Lita. Some, such as Barry Yamutewa (YAH-MOO-TEE-WAH), create both.

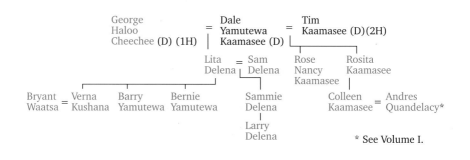

* See Volume I.

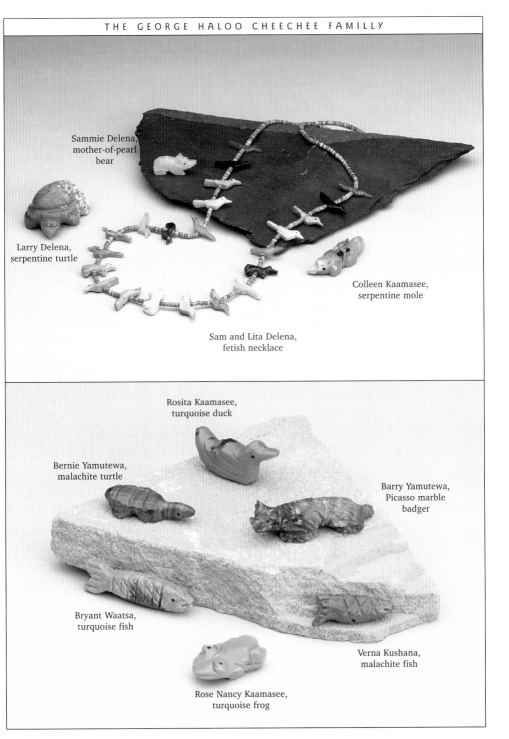

Sammie Delena,
mother-of-pearl
bear

Larry Delena,
serpentine turtle

Sam and Lita Delena,
fetish necklace

Colleen Kaamasee,
serpentine mole

Rosita Kaamasee,
turquoise duck

Bernie Yamutewa,
malachite turtle

Barry Yamutewa,
Picasso marble
badger

Bryant Waatsa,
turquoise fish

Verna Kushana,
malachite fish

Rose Nancy Kaamasee,
turquoise frog

THE HALOO FAMILY

Raymond "Ramie" Haloo,
antler bear (c. 1980s)

Miguel Haloo,
antler bear (c. 1980s)

Raymond "Ramie" Haloo,
antler bear

THIS BRANCH OF THE FAMILY is descended from George Haloo Cheechee and his second wife, Naomi Haloo. Their daughter Tina Sice has recently followed in George's footsteps by producing stringing fetishes. Her late brother Miguel Haloo started carving in the late 1970s and initiated the famous standing-bear style often associated with this family. He passed away in 1990, after teaching many in the later generations to carve. Colvin Peina (PAY-NA) was the first carver of the younger generation that started working in the mid 1980s and has also influenced others. The late Jacob Haloo (George's brother) had several children who are exceptional jewelers, while some descendents are also fetish carvers. In addition to the standing bears, some family members are also known for corn maidens.

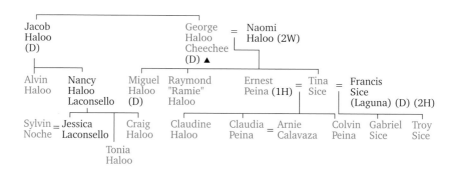

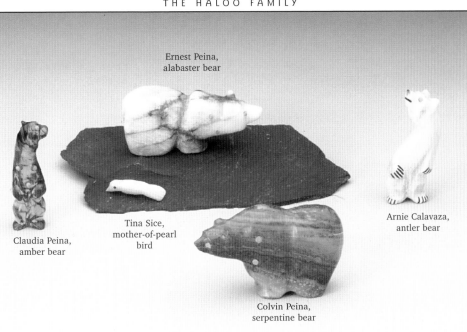

Ernest Peina,
alabaster bear

Claudia Peina,
amber bear

Tina Sice,
mother-of-pearl
bird

Colvin Peina,
serpentine bear

Arnie Calavaza,
antler bear

Craig Haloo,
antler owl

Troy Sice,
antler
corn maiden

Gabriel Sice,
antler
corn maiden

Sylvin Noche,
alabaster owl

Alvin Haloo,
Picasso marble
wolf

Claudine Haloo,
Picasso marble
bear

THE ANDREW EMERSON QUAM AND ROSALIA QUAM FAMILY

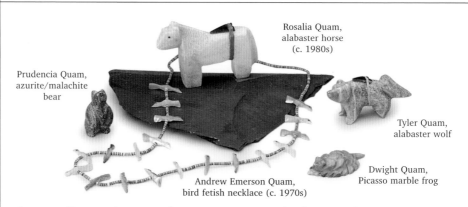

Rosalia Quam, alabaster horse (c. 1980s)

Prudencia Quam, azurite/malachite bear

Tyler Quam, alabaster wolf

Dwight Quam, Picasso marble frog

Andrew Emerson Quam, bird fetish necklace (c. 1970s)

GEORGE HALOO CHEECHEE'S STEPDAUGHTER, the late Rosalia Quam (KWAM), who died in 1989, was known for stringing bird fetishes and for her fetish horses, inlaid frogs, and owls. Both she and her late husband Andrew Emerson Quam (who died in 1978) taught their children the art, as George Haloo Cheechee had taught her. Andrew Emerson was famous for his bird fetish necklaces. The current Quam generation produces a wide range of styles, from fairly realistic to more abstract. Some members are known for specific animals, as Andres Quam for bears or Andrew and Laura Quam for frogs and turtles. Others, such as Prudencia and Tyler Quam, have produced a multiplicity of creatures. Interestingly, the Mahkee (MAH-KEE) sisters Jewelita and Laura have married two of the Quam brothers—Andres and Andrew. Not surprisingly, the sisters and their brother Ulysses have learned fetish carving from the Quams.

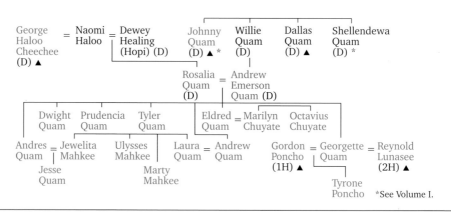

Jewelita Mahkee,
Picasso marble bear

Andres Quam,
dolomite bear

Ulysses Mahkee,
pipestone bear

Andrew and Laura Quam,
mother-of-pearl and turquoise turtle

Jesse Quam,
Picasso marble otter

Eldred Quam,
jet wolf

Tyrone Poncho,
variscite rabbit

Octavius Chuyate,
turquoise horse

Marilyn Chuyate,
serpentine frog

Georgette Quam,
jade turtle

Rosalia Quam,
alabaster horse
(c. 1970s)

Rosalia Quam,
serpentine frog
(c. 1970s)

Rosalia Quam,
antler owl
(c. 1970s)

Rosalia Quam,
serpentine frog
(c. 1970s)

THE LUNASEE, TSETHLIKAI, AND CHAVEZ FAMILIES

TWO CARVING FAMILIES related to the Quandelacys (see Volume I) are the Lunasees (LOO-NA-SEE) and Tsethlikais (TSETH-LIH-KAI). Most carvers in both families produce a similar style of fetish that is somewhat realistic but not heavily detailed. Their diverse animals in a wide range of materials are all very popular. Vernon Lunasee and his brother Ronnie were the first active carvers in their family, starting in the mid 1980s. Vernon was influenced by his ex-wife Prudencia Quam. The two brothers worked with most of their siblings, in addition to a cousin (Fabian Tsethlikai) and an in-law (Terrence Tsethlikai). Several of Terrence's relatives in the Chavez family also make fetishes. David, Jr. and Leroy Chavez were the first, shown by Herbert Him, Sr. (Leroy's ex-brother-in-law), in the late 1980s and then passing on the knowledge to other family members. The Chavez style is a little more simplified than that of the Lunasee family. The three Tsethlikai groups in the family are only distantly related.

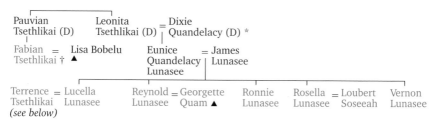

†Francis Tsethlikai (opposite page) is Fabian's cousin.

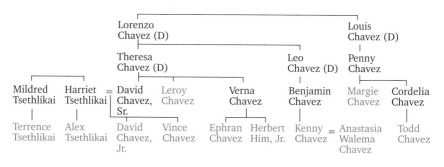

*See Volume I.

42

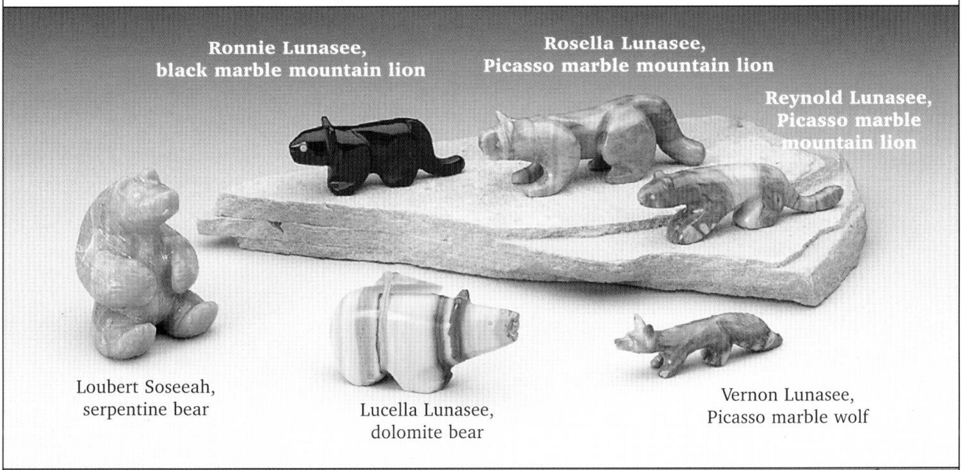

Ronnie Lunasee,
black marble mountain lion

Rosella Lunasee,
Picasso marble mountain lion

Reynold Lunasee,
Picasso marble
mountain lion

Loubert Soseeah,
serpentine bear

Lucella Lunasee,
dolomite bear

Vernon Lunasee,
Picasso marble wolf

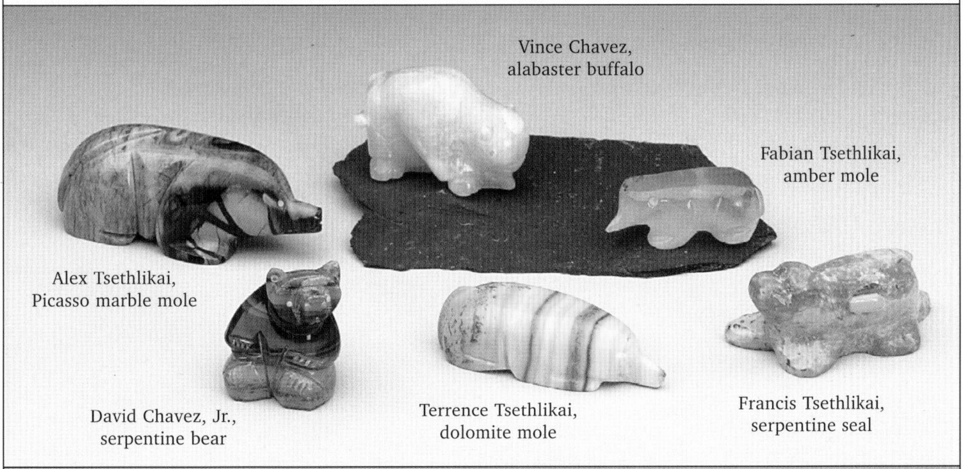

Vince Chavez,
alabaster buffalo

Fabian Tsethlikai,
amber mole

Alex Tsethlikai,
Picasso marble mole

David Chavez, Jr.,
serpentine bear

Terrence Tsethlikai,
dolomite mole

Francis Tsethlikai,
serpentine seal

Todd Chavez,
jet bear

Margie Chavez,
alabaster bear (c. 1980s)

Herbert Him, Jr.,
soapstone dog

Kenny and Anastasia Chavez,
mother-of-pearl mountain lion

Ephran Chavez,
serpentine frog

Leroy Chavez,
marble bear

THE JOHNNY QUAM AND WESTIKA FAMILIES

THE DESCENDENTS of carver Johnny Quam form another important group in the large extended Quam family. Noted jeweler Annie Gasper Quam learned to make fetishes from her father, Johnny. (The work of her sister, Ellen Quandelacy, and the Quandelacy family is discussed in Volume I.) Annie's children also produce both jewelry and carvings. Their fetish style is somewhat reminiscent of that of their Quandelacy cousins, but in the main it is uniquely their own. Her grandson Todd Westika (WES-TIH-KA) was guided in his carving by his maternal aunt, Rhoda Quam, around 1990. His paternal uncle Myron Westika learned from friend Herbert Him. Ellen Quandelacy's granddaughter, Karen Bobelu Hustito (BAH-BEE-LOO HOO-STEE-TOE), was encouraged to continue carving through marriage into the Hustito family, although her father carved stringing and standing fetishes in the past. Because of the widespread nature of this group, their carving styles are quite diverse as well.

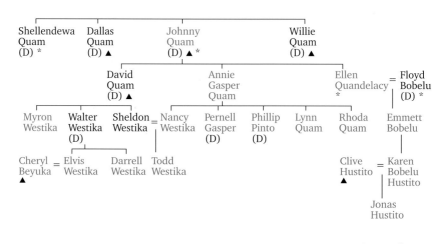

* See Volume I.

Todd Westika,
Picasso marble
buffalo

Rhoda Quam,
azurite coyote

Lynn Quam,
rhodonite coyote

Annie Gasper Quam,
tagua nut turtle

Nancy Westika,
pipestone wolf

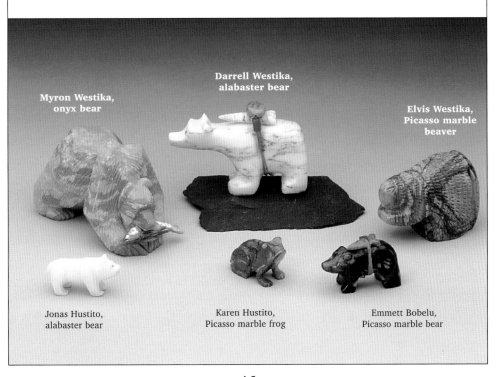

Myron Westika,
onyx bear

Darrell Westika,
alabaster bear

Elvis Westika,
Picasso marble
beaver

Jonas Hustito,
alabaster bear

Karen Hustito,
Picasso marble frog

Emmett Bobelu,
Picasso marble bear

THE HUSTITO & LOWSAYATEE FAMILIES

THE JOINING OF the Hustito and Lowsayatee (LOW-SIGH-TEE) families combined a wide range of carving styles. The late Alonzo Hustito (who died in 1987) was a noted jeweler who also carved fetishes for many years. His son Charles did both as well, starting around 1972. Herbert Hustito was the first family member who gained prominence as a carver, having learned from Dan Quam (see p. 51) in the early 1980s. Herbert then taught his wife, Elfina, and together they helped other family members in developing their art. Most members in their immediate families do more realistic carving. Herbert's nephew Jonathan Natewa, however, makes a different kind of fetish since learning the sgraffito technique from his friend Russell Shack.

Elfina's cousins in the Quam family also do much more streamlined work. Gabriel Quam was the first carver in this branch, starting in the late 1970s. Abby Quam (who began in about 1981) and her husband, Clayton Panteah, work at least partly together on most of their fetishes. Clayton is a phenomenal jeweler and started the inlaying of heartlines into their animals. Cousin Joey Quam was influenced by Colvin Peina's work. As shown on the family tree, this Quam family is related to the Quam families discussed previously through Johnny Quam.

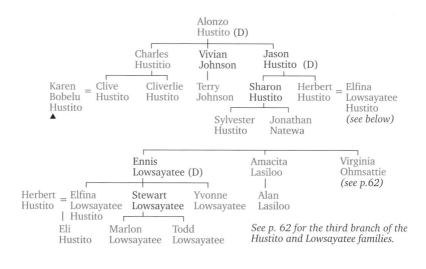

See p. 62 for the third branch of the Hustito and Lowsayatee families.

Alonzo Hustito,
serpentine frog
(c. 1970s)

Clive Hustito,
Picasso marble
buffalo

Cliverlie Hustito,
Picasso marble
corn maiden

Charles Hustito,
turquoise bear

Jonathan Natewa,
black marble buffalo

Herbert Hustito,
antler eagle

Terry Johnson,
antler corn maiden

Sylvester Hustito,
black marble bear

Eli Hustito,
Picasso marble ram

Todd Lowsayatee,
Picasso marble porcupine

Elfina Lowsayatee Hustito,
Picasso marble badger

Marlon Lowsayatee,
antler ram

Yvonne Lowsayatee,
Picasso marble snake

47

Alan Lasiloo,
black marble
bear on
dolomite base

Tony Ohmsattie,
serpentine (with augite)
owl

Virginia Ohmsattie,
jet rabbit

Melissa Quam,
Picasso marble bear

Amacita Lasiloo,
tagua nut buffalo

Gabriel Quam,
alabaster mountain
lion

Huberta Quam,
alabaster bear

Sylvia Quam,
leopard stone
(jasper) rabbit

Robbie Quam Lewis,
travertine seal

Hubert Quam,
pipestone bear

Donovan Quam,
Picasso marble eagle

Roxanne Panteah,
serpentine bear

Joey Quam,
amber bear

Jed Lucio,
purple fluorite bear

Clayton Panteah,
Mexican onyx frog

Abby Quam,
tiger's eye bear

THE NATEWA, LAWEKA, LEONARD, AND DALLAS QUAM FAMILIES

NEIL NATEWA (NAH-TEE-WA) started carving in the early 1950s when he worked for trader Oscar Branson in Albuquerque while at school. He continued with Branson later in Tucson in the early 1960s but stopped producing fetishes by the end of that decade. Neil was famous for standing fetishes (especially bears and frogs), as well as bird stringing fetishes for necklaces. Unfortunately, according to Neil, his pieces were given to other carvers (including other Zuni, non-Zuni, and non-Native Americans) to copy beginning in the late 1960s. Many of these copies have been fraudulently sold as his work. Neil also made jewelry with his wife, Shirley.

The children of Neil's cousins also carve, but each had a different teacher and thus produces diverse styles. LaVies Natewa learned from his wife, Daisy. Staley Natewa and his brother-in-law Travis Lasiloo (LAH-SEE-LOO) were guided by Lance Cheama (CHEE-AH-MA). Among the nieces and nephews of Neil's wife Shirley (through her sister Lorraine), some carve and some make jewelry. Fabian Tsethlikai, husband of Shirley's niece Lisa Bobelu, introduced most of his in-laws who carve to the art. Naturally enough, their fetishes resemble the Lunasee and Tsethlikai carvings.

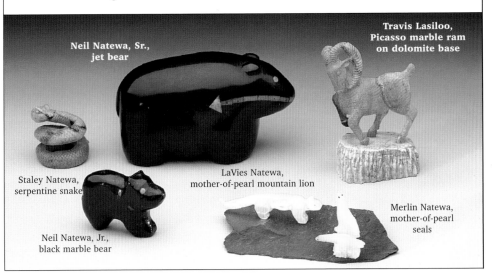

Neil Natewa, Sr., jet bear

Travis Lasiloo, Picasso marble ram on dolomite base

Staley Natewa, serpentine snake

LaVies Natewa, mother-of-pearl mountain lion

Merlin Natewa, mother-of-pearl seals

Neil Natewa, Jr., black marble bear

Daisy Leonard Natewa's extended family includes many artists whose work is more stylized or even harkens back to the "old style" in its simplicity. Daisy learned to carve from ex-husband Andres Quam (see the Andrew and Rosalia Quam family). Many other members were shown the process by Andres or his mother, Rosalia Quam, as well as Daisy. Rosalia's influence can sometimes be seen particularly in their horses. (The Leonard family's original name was Aisetewa [eye-SEE-tee-wa], which was changed to Leonard by the U.S. Government because a member of the family had a first name of Leonard.)

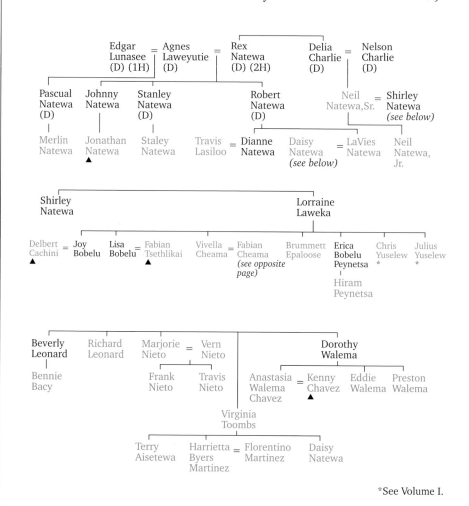

*See Volume I.

Whereas Daisy Natewa's family does primarily traditional carving, Fabian Cheama's family is the driving force behind contemporary work. (Fabian is married to Lorraine Laweka's daughter Vivella.) Fabian's half-brother, Dan Quam, started carving intricately detailed pieces in the early 1980s. Had it not been for him, realistic-style fetishes might not exist today. (This Quam family is also related to the previously mentioned Quams.) Dan showed the rest of his family how to do this exceptional work, and they have gained great fame and won countless awards since then. As noted elsewhere, they have shared their knowledge with many other carvers as well, including their wives, ex-wives, and Banteah cousins. This branch of the family creates a wide range of fetish animals, primarily in Picasso marble and serpentine.

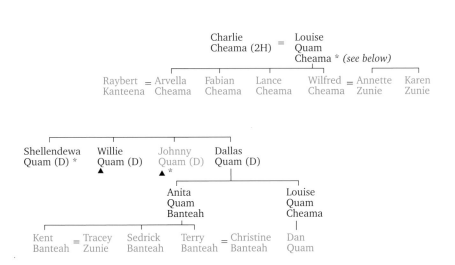

*See Volume I.

Julius Yuselew,
Picasso marble
bear

Hiram Peynetsa,
black marble beaver

Chris Yuselew,
Picasso marble
dinosaur

Brummett Epaloose,
Picasso marble turkey

Vivella Cheama,
Picasso marble horse

Preston Walema,
Picasso marble seal

Bennie Bacy,
Picasso marble wolf

Richard Leonard,
calcite horse

Daisy Natewa,
malachite buffalo

Virginia Toombs,
bone horse

Eddie Walema,
serpentine turtle

Florentino Martinez,
Picasso marble
llama

Vern Nieto,
Picasso marble
eagle

Frank Nieto,
jet squirrel

Marjorie Nieto, serpentine rabbit

Travis Nieto,
alabaster bear

Terry Aisetewa,
sandstone bear

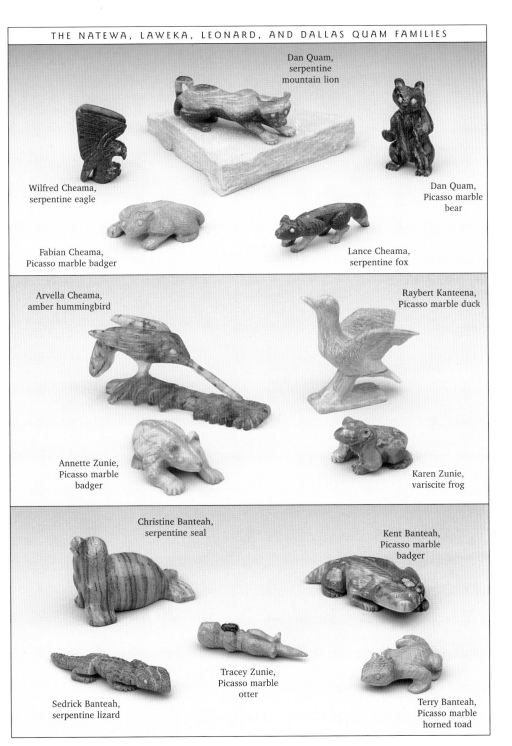

Dan Quam,
serpentine
mountain lion

Wilfred Cheama,
serpentine eagle

Dan Quam,
Picasso marble
bear

Fabian Cheama,
Picasso marble badger

Lance Cheama,
serpentine fox

Arvella Cheama,
amber hummingbird

Raybert Kanteena,
Picasso marble duck

Annette Zunie,
Picasso marble
badger

Karen Zunie,
variscite frog

Christine Banteah,
serpentine seal

Kent Banteah,
Picasso marble
badger

Tracey Zunie,
Picasso marble
otter

Sedrick Banteah,
serpentine lizard

Terry Banteah,
Picasso marble
horned toad

THE LEONARD HALATE FAMILY

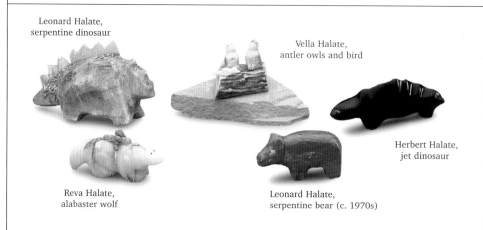

Leonard Halate,
serpentine dinosaur

Vella Halate,
antler owls and bird

Herbert Halate,
jet dinosaur

Reva Halate,
alabaster wolf

Leonard Halate,
serpentine bear (c. 1970s)

THE FETISHES OF LEONARD HALATE (HAH-LAH-TAY) are easily recognized by most collectors. The whimsical feel and almost folk-art quality of his pieces are unmistakable. Leonard started producing on an intermittent basis in the 1940s. He focused primarily on jewelry making in the 1950s before taking up fetish carving seriously in the 1960s. Leonard's unique style continues to influence some of his descendents' work. Others have developed a much sleeker and more rounded look to their fetishes (exemplified by Herbert Halate and Justin Red Elk). The family usually carves in antler, serpentine, jet, pipestone, and zebra stone. Now in his mid 80s, Leonard is one of the oldest active carvers in Zuni.

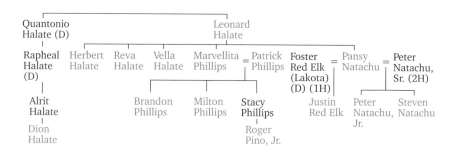

Patrick Phillips,
zebra stone
(marble) bear

Marvellita Phillips,
antler owl and bird

Roger Pino, Jr.,
antler bear

Brandon Phillips,
pipestone snake

Milton Phillips,
dolomite frog

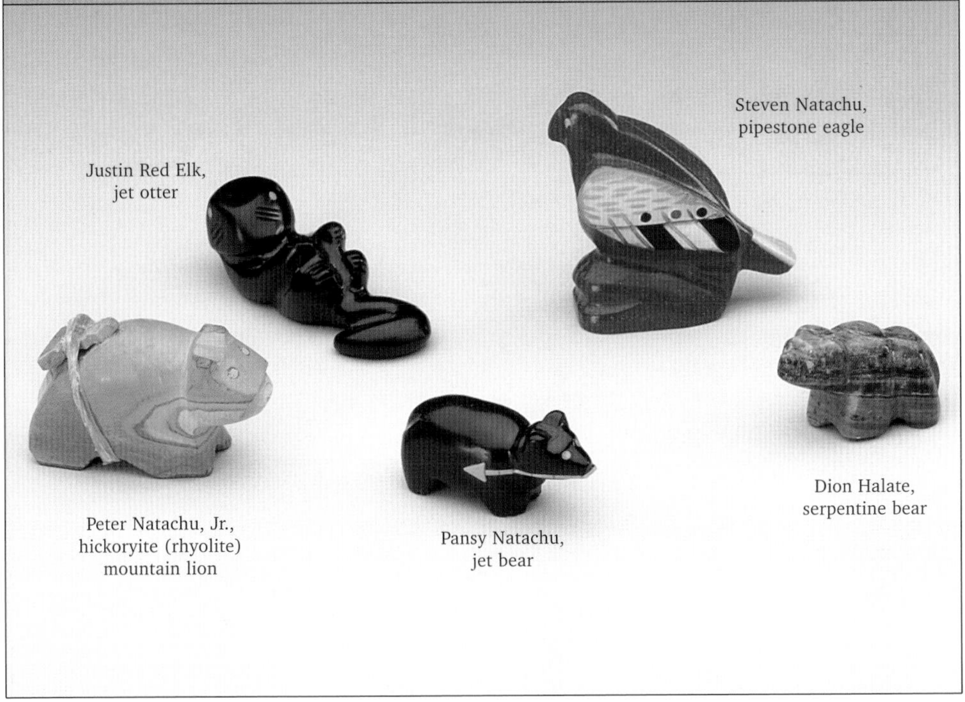

Steven Natachu,
pipestone eagle

Justin Red Elk,
jet otter

Peter Natachu, Jr.,
hickoryite (rhyolite)
mountain lion

Pansy Natachu,
jet bear

Dion Halate,
serpentine bear

THE SEPO PONCHUELLA FAMILY

Sepo Ponchuella,
Ojo rock (argillaceous rock) bear
(c. 1970s)

A JEWELER most of his life, Sepo Ponchuella (who died in 1978) started carving fetishes in his later years. During the 1960s and 70s, he produced bears that were sometimes large and generally made of Ojo rock. For the most part, the art of fetish carving skipped a couple of generations in his family, but now several of his great-grandchildren produce fetishes. Other members of the family continue to make jewelry. Faylena Cachini (KAH-CHIH-NEE) was taught by her ex-husband, Eldred Quam, in the mid 1980s. She guided many of the other carvers in her family. Louise Wallace learned from her ex-husband, Fred Weekoty (WEE-KOE-TEE). Part of the family does very rounded fetishes, while others do fairly angular pieces. Most have a simple, more traditional styling.

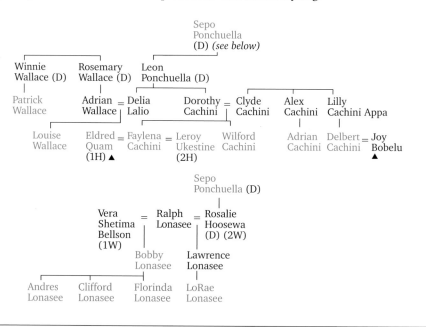

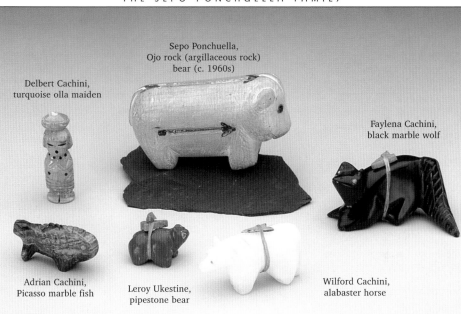

Delbert Cachini,
turquoise olla maiden

Sepo Ponchuella,
Ojo rock (argillaceous rock)
bear (c. 1960s)

Faylena Cachini,
black marble wolf

Adrian Cachini,
Picasso marble fish

Leroy Ukestine,
pipestone bear

Wilford Cachini,
alabaster horse

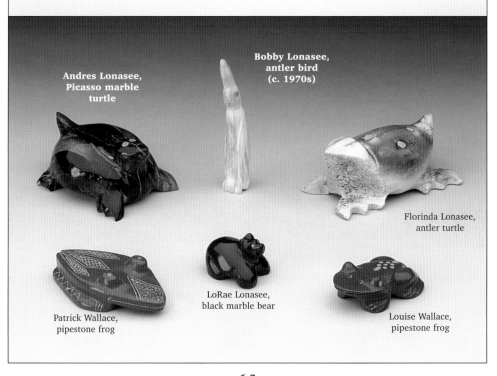

**Andres Lonasee,
Picasso marble
turtle**

**Bobby Lonasee,
antler bird
(c. 1970s)**

Florinda Lonasee,
antler turtle

Patrick Wallace,
pipestone frog

LoRae Lonasee,
black marble bear

Louise Wallace,
pipestone frog

THE PONCHO FAMILY

Gordon Poncho,
dolomite lizard

Todd Poncho,
jet bear

Dan Poncho,
Picasso marble snake

Alex Poncho,
serpentine frog

Stephan Poncho,
pipestone snake

WHILE FEW IN NUMBER, the Ponchos are quite prolific fetish makers. In most carving families, the older members train the younger ones in the art. In this family, Gordon, a member of the younger generation, was the first to carve, starting in the mid 1980s under the tutelage of his (then) wife, Georgette Quam. Gordon's father Dan began producing on his own not long afterwards. All of the family create fetishes with simple clean lines. Some resemble old-style carvings, while others have a more modern flair. Their work is a favorite with collectors.

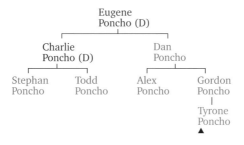

THE BICA AND KALESTEWA FAMILIES

TWO VERY DIFFERENT STYLES of fetishes are produced by the Bica (BEE-KUH) and Kalestewa (KAH-LES-TEE-WAH) sides of the family. The late Simon Bica (who died in 1996) was the first family member to carve, but Rickson Kalestewa, his wife Nellie's grandson, gained the most recognition for his fetishes beginning in the late 1970s. Rickson works primarily in alabaster, producing carvings known for their humorous quality. Other relatives create fetishes in a similar style. Some family members on this side are noted potters, such as Rickson's grandmother, Nellie, and his mother, Quanita.

The Beyuka (BEE-OOH-KAH) family was originally most famous for their beautiful inlay jewelry work, until Cheryl started carving with the help of her husband, Elvis Westika. Cheryl then taught her brother Philbert and son Eli. The work of the Beyukas is generally more contemporary than that of the Kalestewas, and they often produce non-traditional animals.

* See Volume I.

Simon Bica,
alabaster bear

Jack Kalestewa,
alabaster bear

Philbert Beyuka,
zebra stone (marble)
woodpecker
on
wood base

Eli Beyuka,
azurite/chrysocolla
bear

Cheryl Beyuka,
green seasnail shell fish

Rickson Kalestewa,
alabaster bear

Brandon Kalestewa,
alabaster bear

THE SAUL YUSELEW AND HARVEY BEWANIKA FAMILIES

SAUL YUSELEW (YOU-SEE-LOU) first started carving fetishes occasionally as a teenager and then took it up seriously soon after his military service in World War II. He is basically self-taught and probably most famous for his bears, although he makes other animals as well. His style has changed over the years, but each era's carvings have their own traditional charm, nowadays often appearing without eyes. Saul also made jewelry at one time. To the best of my knowledge, at about 85 years of age, Saul is the oldest Zuni carver still producing. His late brother-in-law, Harvey Bewanika (BEE-WAH-NEE-KA), carved as well and was also known for his bears. Note the inlaid "necklaces" that often adorn his fetishes. Only a few other members of Saul's small family carve. His niece, Lorie Yuselew (formerly Lorie Bobelu), learned from her ex-husband, Keith Bobelu.

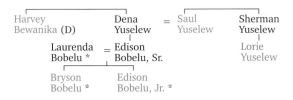

* See Volume I.

Harvey Bewanika,
serpentine bear (c. 1970s)

Lorie Yuselew,
black marble mole

Saul Yuselew,
jet bear (c. 1980s)

Saul Yuselew,
turquoise bear

Saul Yuselew,
serpentine bear (c. 1970s)

Harvey Bewanika,
serpentine bear (c. 1970s)

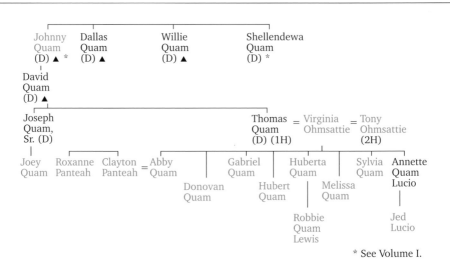

Johnny Quam (D) ▲ *
Dallas Quam (D) ▲
Willie Quam (D) ▲
Shellendewa Quam (D) *

David Quam (D) ▲

Joseph Quam, Sr. (D)

Thomas Quam (D) (1H) = Virginia Ohmsattie = Tony Ohmsattie (2H)

Joey Quam
Roxanne Panteah
Clayton Panteah = Abby Quam
Gabriel Quam
Huberta Quam
Sylvia Quam
Annette Quam Lucio

Donovan Quam
Hubert Quam
Melissa Quam

Robbie Quam Lewis
Jed Lucio

* See Volume I.

BIBLIOGRAPHY

Adair, John
    1944 *The Navajo and Pueblo Silversmiths*. Norman, OK: University of Oklahoma Press.

Harbottle, Garman and Phil C. Weigand
    1992 "Turquoise in Pre-Columbian America," *Scientific American,* Vol. 266, No. 2.

Jernigan, E. Wesley
    1978 *Jewelry of the Prehistoric Southwest*. Albuquerque: School of American Research and University of New Mexico Press.

Kirk, Ruth F.
    1943 *Introduction to Zuni Fetishism*. Santa Fe, NM: Archaeological Institute of America, Papers of the School of American Research.

Rodee, Marian and James Ostler
    1990 *The Fetish Carvers of Zuni*. Albuquerque: The Maxwell Museum of Anthropology, University of New Mexico.

Schumann, Walter
    1991 *Minerals of the World*. New York: Sterling Publishing Company.

Tindall, James R., Annette Rogers, and Eric Deeson
    1973 *The Collector's Encyclopedia of Rocks and Minerals*. Edited by A. F. L. Deeson. New York: Clarkson N. Potter, Inc.

Zeitner, June Culp
    1996 *Gem and Lapidary Materials for Cutters, Collectors, and Jewelers*. Tucson, AZ: Geo Science Press, Inc.

INDEX

ABOUT THE AUTHOR

Kent McManis became interested in Zuni fetishes in the mid 1960s when a trader friend presented him with his first bear fetishes. (He later discovered they were carved by noted artist Theodore Kucate.) Kent began his own Native American arts and crafts business in the early 1970s and met his wife Laurie when she came into the store as a customer soon afterwards. Laurie was the catalyst for their fetish collecting. Kent and Laurie own Grey Dog Trading Company in Tucson, Arizona.